My Story, Our Fight:

A Powerful, Faith Inspired Memoir of Endometriosis, With Spiritual Fighting Tips to Keep Women in The Ring of Life.

By

Jessica Carter

I dedicate this book to the Lord. I will forever be your willing servant. This book is your work done through my hands.

From one sister to another,
You are not alone.

I pray that this book blesses and strengthens you in your suffering. I pray that you will see yourself in this book and find comfort, peace, and healing. I decree and declare that as you read angels are being released to minister to your very need. I pray a fresh anointing over every doctor assigned to your life. I pray that God blesses the work of their hands and that they operate in wisdom and precision.
I prophecy healing and medical breakthroughs.
Amen.

Photography by Melodee Joy
Edited by Amanda Violet Christensen

Printed in the United States of America

First Printing: Jan 2019
Kindle

ISBN-9781791771744

Contents

Introduction

Approximately 176 million women worldwide are impacted by endometriosis, and an estimated 1 out of 10 women suffer in the United States. If you are reading this book, it is probably because like me, you are one out of the 176 million women. Or it is because you know someone that has been diagnosed and you are searching for ways to try to understand and support them. You have chosen the right book. You will find that this book will provide insight into what we have experienced and strategies to help support someone navigating through it. I am not here to be a doctor and explain what endometriosis is, its signs, symptoms, and treatment. I am writing to share my experiences and offer hope to what often times seems like a hopeless situation.

Pain has been my primary motivation behind this book. My pastor says, "Every season serves you." I want to take this revelation a step further. I believe that not only does every season serve you, every situation serves you. I believe that it is all about perspective and positioning. What is your position with endometriosis? Are you the victim or victor? One day, I decided that I no longer wanted to be a victim of my circumstances and allow this thing to defeat, discourage, and take my life away. I decided that I would walk in victory while I wait on my healing to manifest. I decided to partner with pain and allow it to be the fuel that serves me as I write page by page, and chapter by chapter.

So, to the woman that feels like you can't go another day in pain...YOU CAN! To the woman that feels like you can't fight any more...YOU CAN! Keep fighting! Lastly, to the woman that is questioning where God is in the midst of this pain and wondering whether or not He can hear your prayers and cries for help: He is right there with you. Yes, He hears your prayers and cries for help. How do I know? Because the Bible says He collects our tears. I am telling you that your very tears have been the water that allowed every word for this book to come into fruition.

God wants you healed and whole. In Luke 8:43-48 we read about a woman who suffered with a blood issue for twelve years. She had spent all her livelihood on physicians and could not be healed by any doctor. She touched the boarder of Jesus garment and immediately her flow of blood stopped. Jesus said, "Who touched me?" The disciples said there were multitudes of people pressing against, but Jesus knew it was somebody in particular. The woman came forth and declared that it was her that had touched Him and how she was healed immediately. And he said to her, "Daughter, be of good comfort: thy faith hath made thee whole; go in peace" (Luke 8:48 KJV). What this text tells me is that my faith can't be in doctors and medicine alone. This also tells me that I should not just pursue physical healing, I should pursue wholeness. A biblical definition of wholeness is the state of being perfectly well in body, soul (mind, will, and emotions) and spirit. The text states that the woman was healed immediately after she touched Jesus garment and yet, Jesus stated in verse 48 "thy faith has made thee whole".

Some will read this book and think that it is just another book. Some will read half of the book and then put it in a pile with the rest of the books you haven't finished. But, for some people, or just one person, this book will be the very thing that activates your faith and stirs you into action.

The woman with the issue of blood pressed her way to where she knew Jesus would be and then pressed her way through the crowd just to touch Him. What have you done to seek out healing? What are you willing to do to not only be healed, but to be whole?

Bathroom Chronicles

I remember being in the bathroom screaming, while clinching the toilet paper roll and my butt at the same time, hoping to somehow stop myself from having to use the bathroom. Sometimes the pain renders you speechless and all you can do is scream. I wish I could say this was just one experience. I wish I could say that this was something I could go to the doctor for, get a pill, and then it disappears. This happened multiple times and there is no single, lucky pill. Every month when it was time for my menstrual cycle, I had to brace myself for what was about to happen, knowing that in reality there is absolutely nothing I could ever do to prepare myself for the pain I would soon experience. In my mind I would always imagine myself being a pilot and yelling out "Brace for Impact!" But instead of talking to passengers, I was talking to my body. Now, I have never been a pilot, and I have never been on a plane that was about to crash. However, I imagine the same panic and fear they must feel in that moment, I felt. I imagine the same way one would grip the seat trying to hold on for dear life, is the same way I have gripped the toilet seat holding on for dear life. I imagine the same screams as you watch the plane go down knowing that there is nothing that you can do but brace yourself is that same screams I cried out knowing that my body was about to take a hit but that I would survive. This is a result of endometriosis being on my bladder and my bowels.

Spiritual Fighting Tip: FAITH

I pondered on this tip for months trying to find the right words to say and the truth is there are none. There are times in life and situations we face that renders us speechless. The truth is my screams became my prayers in those moments. It is only one word that got me through and one word that still gets me through to this day: FAITH. My faith teaches me that if I believe in healing, then I will receive healing. My faith teaches me that no weapon formed against me shall prosper.

Being a Christian does not make me exempt from sickness and pain. So, if endometriosis is the weapon that has been formed against me, I shall fear not because it will not prosper. My faith teaches me that I have victory and authority over critical illness and disease.

My faith is my ability to believe beyond doubt that not only *will the pain not always last,* [**the pain is temporary**] but that I will be healed and whole one day. One thing that I have learned in life is that we all have faith. We have faith in our jobs, cars, houses, and relationships. So, I dare not ask the question: where is your faith? According to Hebrews 11:1 faith is the substance of things hoped for, the evidence of things not seen. Could it be that we have ran out of the very substance needed to hope and believe in healing, because our faith, has been misplaced, in all the wrong things. We need faith for the things we can't see.

Pain

Countless times I have found myself in this place. I recall walking through the automatic sliding doors wishing I could really run through the doors to the desk in hopes that it would make my process faster so that I would be one step closer to relief. Somehow the pain drowned out the sounds and smells, but I could feel despair roaming through the building. I sat in the thin padded seats that offered little comfort, twisting and squirming. I stared down at the floor because holding my head up would mean holding my body in an upright position, which at times was all too painful. I remember the nurse calling out my name, "Jessica Carter" and my body responding before I could. Somehow just the sound of my name gave me enough strength to get up and walk to the back. The triage nurse asking those daunting questions, "what brings you here today? Are you allergic to anything? When did this start? On a level of 1 to 10 with 10 being the highest, where is your pain right now?" BEYOND THE SCALE!! Is that an answer? In my smart, sarcastic voice. Now, before you go judging me, sisters I'm sure we can all agree that every now and then you say some things that shouldn't be said, or you say things the wrong way. The struggle is real. Seriously! In those moments even though I was answering questions I was also trying to silence the voice of pain, that at the time felt like it was trying to out talk me. It's almost as if every cramp has an echo. So, you feel the pain in your reproductive system, but you hear the echo from there to all throughout your body until it reaches your brain. There would be times when one shot would work, and times when it didn't, and they had to pull out the big guns, and by that, I mean "Morphine." For those that may be wondering why we must go to the emergency room so often, instead of seeing the doctor: Endometriosis pain doesn't know or understand time. Doctors are limited to what they can prescribe and the dosage when you are at home and outside of their care.

Pills

I allowed pills to become my counselor and pain my companion. This happened because I started talking to the pain more than I talked to God. We bonded during the most painful times. He was there when I could barely walk. He was there when the heating pad would give out on me. He stayed up with me throughout the restless nights. When I cried, he became my pillow to lean on. And, when I felt I needed help he told me to make an appointment with Pills.

Hello Pills, my name is Jessica. It's so nice to meet you, Pain told me all about you. He said that if anybody could help me, it was you.

"Well, I sure hope so. Let's start by you telling me what's going on."

Well, today is one of those painful days. I feel him in my sleep. I feel him as I go throughout my day. Sometimes he causes me trouble when I'm just trying to walk. My ovaries know him best. He weakens my body and sometimes makes it feel impossible to function.

"I see, how long has this been going on?"

Well, now that I think about it, we started getting to know each other back in middle school but, we got really close right after high school. So, let's say about 17 years. So, as you can see I really need your help.

"I see! Well, I'm going to give you some homework and I would like to start you on some pills that will make you forget all about Pain."

I continued my sessions with Pills for months and months. Instead of leading me along a path to healing and wholeness like a good counselor, it was leading me down a path of deception and emptiness.

Spiritual Fighting Tip: PURPOSE

In life outside of my pursuit of God there was only ever one thing I focused on. I remember asking God from a very young age, "what is my purpose? Why did you create me?"

I learned early on that everything living, moving, and operating has a purpose. The trees have purpose. Animals have a purpose. The sun has a purpose. Cars have a purpose. Houses have purpose. So, what is mine, God? Years would go by and I would still be asking the same questions.

It wasn't until my 20's that I realized I shouldn't just ask my creator, I should ask and pursue Him. In my pursuit and discovery of God I found my identity and discovered my purpose. But, it didn't stop there, what I realized is that purpose is something that God continues to reveal. He would give me one puzzle piece at a time, and piece by piece my life began to come together. I began doing things I never thought I could or would ever do, but somehow it felt like exactly what I was born to do. Life was no longer just life, I was on purpose with purpose. Who would have known that in my pursuit of God and discovery of purpose, it would be one of the number one things that saved my life when I came face to face with endometriosis. Purpose keeps me in the ring when the battle gets rough, and I feel like I can't take another hit. When I feel like endometriosis is cornering me in and I can't see a way out, purpose gives me fresh vision.

This book is the result of me not just finding purpose but finding purpose in my pain. It kept me from being addicted to pain pills. When I felt like I couldn't work, it kept me on the job because I knew I needed to fund the things that God called me to do. There is no greater responsibility than that of pursuing purpose. People's lives depend on you doing the thing you were born to do. Knowing that people needed to hear a word from the Lord through me.

Knowing that people needed my intercession. Knowing that people looked to me for answers and direction. Focus on purpose. Pills are not your friend. Addiction is not your friend....... Purpose is!

Divine Encounter

One day I woke up like normal, took a shower, brushed my teeth, washed my face, and got dressed for work. I had a doctor's appointment that day and afterwards a meeting with my recruiter. I was about to make one of the biggest steps in my life. I was all signed up for the military and ready to go to boot camp. There was one thing standing in the way, my period pain. At the time I was on the Depo shot to prevent me from having a cycle, because my doctors didn't know what to do about my pain and symptoms. My recruiter said that I wouldn't be able to be on the Depo shot during basic training which meant I had to go to the doctor to try and figure out what to do about my pain. Because I knew I wouldn't make it one day in boot camp with the pain I experienced on my cycle. So, I made up in my mind I was going to the doctor and he was going to have to figure it out what was wrong because I WAS GOING to the military.

I walked into the doctor's office with a different strut, one that said I meant business. They did all the normal stuff that they do and then the doctor enters the room. "Doctor," I said. "Listen here, you are going to have to figure out what's going on with me because I am about to leave, and I can't take this birth control while I'm gone, that you only gave to me because you didn't know what to do about my pain and symptoms." So, I give him a run-down of my symptoms as if he doesn't already know and proceeded to say I need answers.

The look on his face appeared that he understood my seriousness or either he thought I was crazy. He left the room and then something happened. Something I had never experienced that shifted my entire life. As he left the room, someone else entered. I looked up and there before me was a woman dressed in colorful scrubs with solid colored Dansko shoes. She appeared to be normal but when she began to speak, I knew something was different. She said, "I couldn't help but over hear what you are going through." She said, "I'm not supposed to do this, but I know a doctor that can help you. My daughter deals with the same thing." She proceeded to write, on a small piece of paper because that's all she had on her, the name and number of her daughter's doctor. The doctor came back in the room and the rest was a blur. I didn't know at the time, but I had just experienced my first divine encounter.

All throughout the bible you will see instances where angels showed up in human form to deliver a message or an answer to God's people. She delivered the answer to my prayer. I called and made an appointment, and as soon as I told this new doctor what was going on he said, "you need to have surgery immediately." Turns out he was right, I had surgery a week later and the problem was what he thought it was: I was medically diagnosed with endometriosis. While I never got the chance to go and fight for my country, I began the journey of an ongoing battle. I became a solider and my body the battle field.

Spiritual Fighting Tip: PRAYER

"Don't worry about anything but pray about everything. With thankful hearts offer up your prayers and requests to God," (Philippians 4:6 CEV). At first glance of this text you are probably thinking what I thought when I read it or hear someone quote it time after time. You're probably thinking, "Yea, yea, I know I'm supposed to just pray, and talk to this invisible God, and believe that everything will be just fine." Well, yes and no.

When you look further you will see that the text is suggesting you do a lot more. According to Dictionary.com, worry means "to give way to anxiety or unease; allow one's mind to dwell on difficulty or troubles." So, the definition brings more clarity to what the text is instructing us to do. "Don't worry" means, don't give way to things that causes me anxiety it unease. Don't allow my mind to dwell on difficulty or troubles. So, in essence I would have things, difficulties, and troubles that would worry me, but my responsibility is to not let it worry me. The second part of the text is the how. How do I not worry? How do I not dwell on my troubles? How do I not dwell on my pain? How do I not give in to the worries that endometriosis brings? I do that by praying. Prayer is simply communicating with God. It's simple but powerful.

I open my mouth to talk to God; and because He has given power to my tongue, when I ask or say a thing, it must happen. When I open my mouth to pray, I am giving my angels an assignment and putting them to work. When I open my mouth to pray, the words I release causes a shift to happen in the earth, and in the atmosphere, and world I know begins to respond accordingly. I prayed for my doctors and asked for specifics pertaining to my every need. "God, I need a doctor that is anointed, one that not only has the knowledge and training, but one that knows your voice and instruction. God, I need a doctor that is not just skilled in surgery, but I need one that is skilled in pain management and a total health plan. One that is knowledgeable about the latest medicines and treatments. One that has a heart for endometriosis."

I prayed and asked these things over and over, and over time I begin to get the help I needed. I had another divine encounter as I was writing this book. I was enrolled in a program and I felt drawn and connected to one of my teachers. I pressed into the leading and unction of the Holy Spirit and it turns out she had the very same thing I was sitting in her class struggling with. She knew my pain and became yet another angel in the earth that held the answer to my prayers. She did not know this but at the time my other doctor had just told me there was nothing else he could do for me. She connected me with a female doctor that is a believer and had previously suffered with endometriosis. When life brings you troubles, which it will, pray and don't worry.

'Til death do us part

In December 2017, I was shockingly uprooted from the home and life that I knew and was forced to move back home. I remember it just like it was yesterday. It was the week before Christmas, when two extremely long text messages came through as I drove home from work. I remember pulling over because I couldn't believe my eyes. This can't be real!! My eyes began to water. My heart dropped. My stomach began to do flips and tricks that I had never felt. It was as if I got one of those dreadful calls saying someone near and dear to me had passed away. I bent over the stirring wheel and felt death come over me. It wasn't death as you know it. It was the death of my marriage. When I came back to myself I began to blow up his phone with sheer desperation to save my marriage. No answer.

I kept calling, begging him to pick up and talk to me. He answered but his mind was made up. He wanted me out the house by the end of the weekend, but I stayed for the week in hopes of finding an apartment to move into instead of going back home.

Just months before this, October to be exact, I had visited my doctor to follow-up from another emergency room visit. I had just had surgery in February of that year, but somehow the endometriosis had grown back with a vengeance. He said its back and its bad! He was desperate to try me on hormonal therapy medications to prevent the rapid growth. This medicine was one I had dreaded for years. The medicine bottle reads "Chemo Therapy Treatment," and my heart just sank. I have no choice, I had to keep repeating to myself. It's going to be ok. This medicine will make you better. I'll do anything to prevent another surgery so soon.

Oh, the thoughts that ran through my mind. I mustered up enough strength and faith to start the medicine. My bowels began to lock. My fingers began tingling. Sharp pains ran through my arms and began to make normal movement feel impossible at times. I went through all of that while being separated. Yes, we separated, got back together and then weeks later he asked for a divorce. The separation was my choice, I had always wanted nothing more than to make my marriage work. But when the endometriosis took a turn for the worst, I had to make a decision. Him or me? I knew that I no longer had enough strength to fight the endometriosis, fight for my marriage and fight the demons he chose to wrestle with. See, what I just described to you was just the first round of treatment that I had to stop abruptly because of the symptoms. My doctor said, "let's try another treatment," but it was the same kind of medication, and unfortunately, I experienced the same symptoms. My treatment plan had failed and so had my marriage. When I decided to separate it was never with divorce in mind. When I made the decision to choose me or him, it was really about choosing life over death. My body had had enough. My mind had had enough. Spiritually I had had enough. Emotionally, I was broken and depleted.

A month went by and I began to feel better and stronger. My husband began to come around again and we ended up back together just in enough time for Thanksgiving. He convinced me he was different. He convinced me that the cheating was a lie. He convinced me that his mind was made up and I was what he wanted. My heart began to turn back towards him and I let him in again. Fast-forward three weeks later is where this chapter started. Sickness and disease do not give you a break during difficult times. In fact, it's when you are stressed and worried that typically makes the flair ups and pain worse.

Spiritual Fighting Tip: SUPPORT

The greatest fighters are not great because of themselves. What makes them great is the team of people that support them. You need the right coach, physical fitness trainers, doctors, and a group of people that love you regardless of whether your winning or losing. My team consists of Pastors, Counselors, Doctors, Intercessors, My Mother, Sisters, Brothers, and a countless number of spiritual brothers and sisters. When I feel as though I don't have the words to pray the Holy Spirit makes intercession for me. When I have the strength to call on my Pastor or sisters, they pray and respond with encouragement or counsel. When I go to the emergency room, the intercessors at my church are interceding for me. When I feel like victory is getting blurry, I'm reminded of 2 Kings 6:16-17. You are not alone, there is an army of angels fighting with you.

Knock Out Rounds

I f you have made it this far in the book it means that you have enough stamina and you're ready for the knockout rounds. This portion of the book will consist of *scriptures* and *declarations* to use for prayer and strength.

Strength

"Proclaim this among the nations: Prepare war! Stir up the mighty men! Let all the men of war draw near, let them come up. Beat your plowshares into swords, and your pruning hooks into spears; **let the weak say, I am strong [a warrior]**!"

-Joel 3:9-10 AMPC

"I can do all things **through Christ** which strengthens me."

-Philippians 4:13 NIV

"But you belong to God, my dear children. You have already won a victory over those people, because the Spirit who **lives in you is greater** than the spirit who **lives in the world.**"

-1 John 4:4 NLT

"No, in all these things we are **more than conquerors** through him who loved us."

-Romans 8:37 NIV

"And he said unto me, My grace is sufficient for thee: for my **strength is made perfect in weakness**. Most gladly therefore will I rather glory in my infirmities, that the power of Christ may rest upon me."

-2 Corinthians 12:9 KJV

"I pray that **out of the riches of His glory**, He may **strengthen you with powe**r through His Spirit in your inner being,"

-Ephesians 3:16 BSB

"Keep actively watching and praying that you may not come into temptation; the spirit is willing, but the flesh is weak."

-Matthew 26:41 AMP

Faith

"You don't have enough faith," Jesus told them. "I tell you the truth, **if you had faith even as small as a mustard seed**, you could say to this mountain, 'Move from here to there,' and it would move. Nothing would be impossible."

-Matthew 17:20 NLT

"Jesus responded, "Why are you afraid? You have so little faith!" Then he got up and rebuked the wind and waves, and suddenly there was a great calm."

-Matthew 8:26 NLT

"For I consider [from the standpoint of faith] that the sufferings of the present life are not worthy to be compared with the glory that is about to be revealed to us *and* in us!"

-Romans 8:18 AMP

"Strength and honour *are* her clothing; and she shall rejoice in time to come."

-Proverbs 31:25 KJV

"This is my command--be strong and courageous! Do not be afraid or discouraged. For the LORD your God is with you wherever you go."

-Joshua 1:9 NLT

"Faith is **the confidence** that what we **hope for will actually happen**; it gives us **assurance** about things **we cannot see**."

-Hebrews 11:1 NLT

"Who through faith conquered kingdoms, administered justice, and gained what was promised; who shut the mouths of lions, quenched the fury of the flames, and escaped the edge of the sword; whose weakness was turned to strength; and who became powerful in battle and routed foreign armies."

-Hebrews 11:33-34 NIV

Authority

"And he called the twelve together and gave them power and authority over all demons and to cure diseases, and he sent them out to proclaim the kingdom of God and to heal."

-Luke 9:1-2 ESV

"Listen carefully: I have given you authority [that you now possess] to tread on [a]serpents and scorpions, and [the ability to exercise authority] over all the power of the enemy (Satan); and nothing will [in any way] harm you."

-Luke 10:19 AMP

"No weapon that is formed against you shall prosper; and every tongue that shall rise against you in judgment you shall condemn. This is the heritage of the servants of the LORD, and their righteousness is of me, said the LORD."

-Isaiah 54:17 AKJV

"Yea, though I walk through the valley of the shadow of death, I will fear no evil: for thou art with me; thy rod and thy staff they comfort me."

–Psalm 23:4 KJV

"And God blessed them, and God said unto them, Be fruitful, and multiply, and replenish the earth, and subdue it: and have dominion over the fish of the sea, and over the fowl of the air, and over every living thing that moveth upon the earth."

–Genesis 1:28 KJV

"Therefore, take up the full armor of God, so that you will be able to resist in the evil day, and having done everything, to stand firm."

–Ephesians 6:13 NASB

"The weapons we fight with are not the weapons of the world. On the contrary, they have divine power to demolish strongholds. We demolish arguments and every pretension that sets itself up against the knowledge of God, and we take captive every thought to make it obedient to Christ."

-2 Corinthians 10:4-5 NIV

Peace

"I have told you all this so that you may have peace in me. Here on earth you will have many trials and sorrows. But take heart, because I have overcome the world."

-John 16:33 NLT

"Don't worry about anything, but pray about everything. With thankful hearts offer up your prayers and requests to God."

-Philippians 4:6 CEV

"Truly he is my rock and my salvation; he is my fortress, I will never be shaken."

-Psalm 62:2 NIV

"In the same way, the Spirit helps us in our weakness. We do not know what we ought to pray for, but the

Spirit himself intercedes for us through wordless groans.27 And he who searches our hearts knows the mind of the Spirit, because the Spirit intercedes for God's people in accordance with the will of God."

-Romans 8:26-27 NIV

"And the peace of God, which passeth all understanding, shall keep your hearts and minds through Christ Jesus."

-Philippians 4:7 KJV

"The LORD gives **strength** to **his people**; the LORD **blesses his people** with **peace**."

-Psalm 29:11 NIV

"Thou wilt keep *him* in **perfect peace**, *whose* **mind** *is* **stayed** *on thee*: because **he trusteth in thee**."

-Isaiah 26:3 KJV

Healing

"O Lord my God, I cried to You, and You healed me."

-Psalm 30:2 KJV

"He forgives all my sins and heals all my diseases."

-Psalm 103:3 NLT

"My son, pay attention to what I say; turn your ear to my words. Do not let them out of your sight, keep them within your heart; for they are life to those who find them and health to one's whole body."

-Proverbs 4:20-22 NIV

"Great crowds came to him, bringing the lame, the blind, the crippled, the mute and many others, and laid them at his feet; and he healed them. The people were amazed when they saw the mute speaking, the crippled made well, the lame walking and the blind seeing. And they praised the God of Israel."

-Matthew 15:30-31 NIV

"Is anyone among you sick? Let him call for the elders of the church, and let them pray over him, anointing him with oil in the name of the Lord. And the prayer of faith will save the sick, and the Lord will raise him up. And if he has committed sins, he will be forgiven."

-James 5:14-16 NKJV

"But [in fact] He has borne our griefs,
And He has carried our sorrows *and* pains;
Yet we [ignorantly] assumed that He was stricken,
Struck down by God and degraded *and* humiliated [by Him].
But He was wounded for our transgressions,
He was crushed for our wickedness [our sin, our injustice, our wrongdoing];
The punishment [required] for our well-being *fell* on Him,
And by His stripes (wounds) we are healed."

-Isaiah 53:4-5 AMP

"The ropes of death entangled me; floods of destruction swept over me. The grave wrapped its ropes around me; death laid a trap in my path. But in my distress I cried out to the Lord; yes, I prayed to my God for help. He heard me from his sanctuary; my cry to him reached his ears."

Psalm 18:4-6 NLT

Declarations

I decree and declare that I am strong.

I decree and declare that I can do ALL things through Christ.

I decree and declare that Christ is my strength.

I decree and declare that I have victory.

I decree and declare that He that is in ME is GREATER than He that lives in the world.

I decree and declare that I AM more than a CONQUEROR.

I decree and declare that in MY WEAKNESS Christ strength is made perfect.

I decree and declare that the POWER of CHRIST rest upon ME.

I decree and declare that MY INNER being is strengthened through His spirit.

I decree and declare that MY SPIRIT is STRONG.

I decree and declare that my faith is enough.

I decree and declare that I have MOUNTAIN MOVING.
POWER in my tongue.

Endometriosis I command you to move now in Jesus
name.

I decree and declare that NOTHING is IMPOSSIBLE if I
believe.

I rebuke pain and decree and declare my body is calm.

I decree and declare that I am clothed in strength.

I decree and declare that I am strong and courageous.

I decree and declare that I am free of fear and
discouragement.

I decree and declare that the Lord is with me, I AM not
ALONE.

I decree and declare that I will believe despite of what it
looks like.

I decree and declare that I will believe despite of what
my body feels like.

I decree and declare that I have power.

I decree and declare that I have authority.

I decree and declare that I have healing power.

I decree and declare that I have authority over sickness.

I decree and declare that no weapon (endometriosis) formed against me shall prosper.

I decree and declare that I HAVE DOMINION.

I decree and declare that I am clothed with the full armor of God.

I decree and declare that everything that exalts itself up against the knowledge of God is demolished.

I decree and declare that I have overcome _____.

I decree and declare that the Lord is my rock and my salvation.

I decree and declare that the Lord is my fortress.

I decree and declare that I will not be shaken or moved.

I decree and declare that peace guards my heart and mind.

I decree and declare that I am healed.

I decree and declare that the word of the Lord is written in my heart.

I decree and declare that the word of the Lord is medicine to my whole body.

I decree and declare that Jesus was wounded for my transgressions, crushed for my wickedness, my punishment fell on Him, and by His stripes I AM HEALED.

I decree and declare that my cry has reached His ears.

References

Amplified Bible (AMP). Bible Gateway,
    www.biblegateway.com. Accessed 15 Jul. 2018.

Contemporary English Version (CEV). Bible Gateway,
    www.biblegateway.com. Accessed 15 Jul. 2018.

English Standard Version (ESV). Bible Gateway,
    www.biblegateway.com. Accessed 15 Jul. 2018.

Kings James Version (KJV). Bible Gateway,
    www.biblegateway.com. Accessed 15 Jul. 2018.

New American Standard Bible (NASB). Bible Gateway,
    www.biblegateway.com. Accessed 15 Jul. 2018.

New International Version (NIV). Bible Gateway,
    www.biblegateway.com. Accessed 15 Jul. 2018.

New King James Version (NKJV). Bible Gateway,
    www.biblegateway.com. Accessed 15 Jul. 2018.

New Living Translation (NLT). Bible Gateway,
    www.biblegateway.com. Accessed 15 Jul. 2018.

Made in the USA
Columbia, SC
19 April 2022

59192124R00026